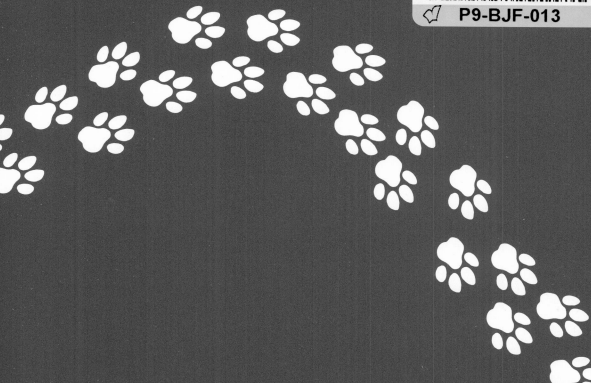

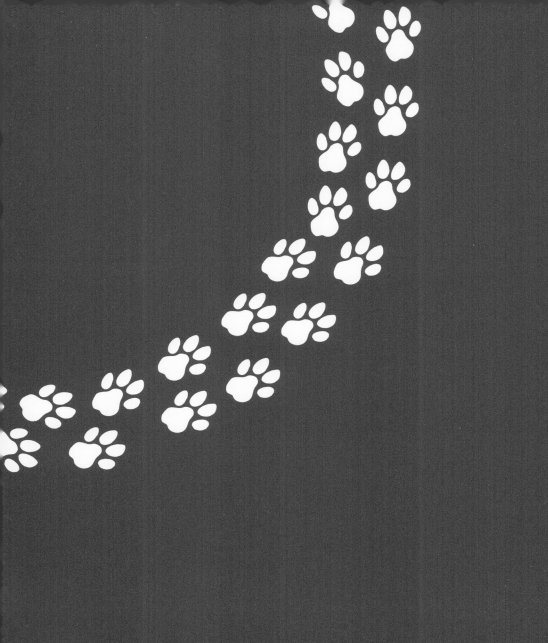

Puppies, Puppies Everywhere!

Puppies, Puppies Everywhere!

Written by
Peggy Schaefer

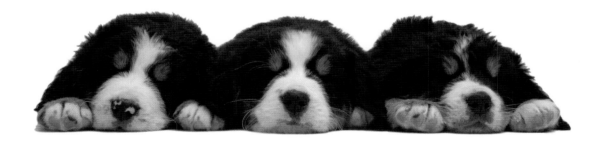

Ideals Publications   Nashville, Tennessee

ISBN 0-8249-5887-X

Published by Ideals Publications
A division of Guideposts
535 Metroplex Drive, Suite 250
Nashville, Tennessee 37211
www.idealsbooks.com

Color separations by Precision Color Graphics, Franklin, Wisconsin

Printed and bound in Italy by LEGO

Designed by Marisa Calvin

Front jacket photograph: Noriyuki Yoshida/SuperStock
Back jacket photograph: Stock Connection Distribution/Alamy
Jacket flap photograph: age fotostock/SuperStock

1 3 5 7 9 10 8 6 4 2

Whoever said you
can't buy happiness
forgot about
little puppies.
—Gene Hill

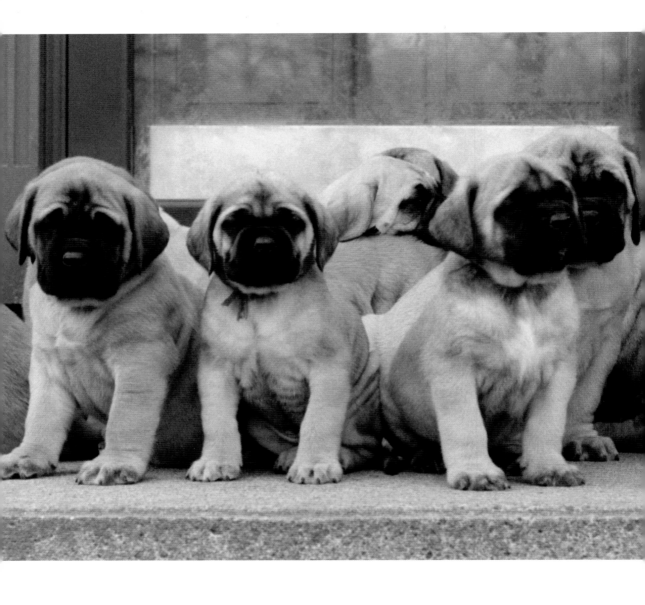

Puppies,
puppies
everywhere,

sometimes
one,

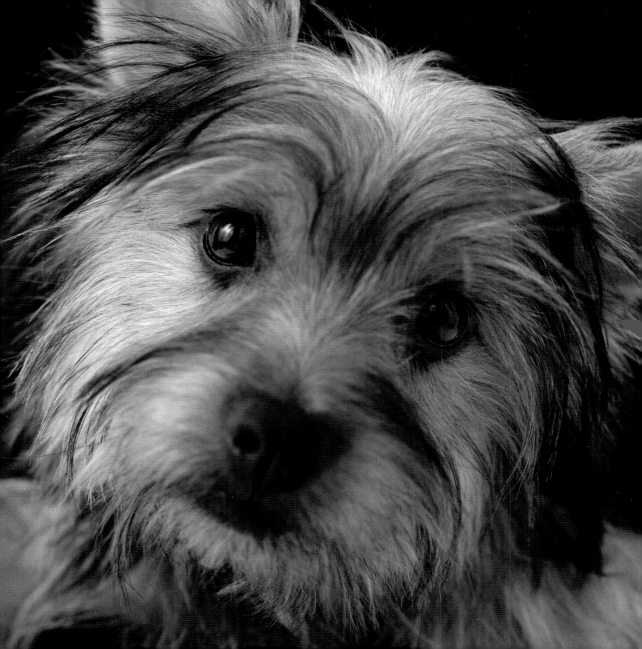

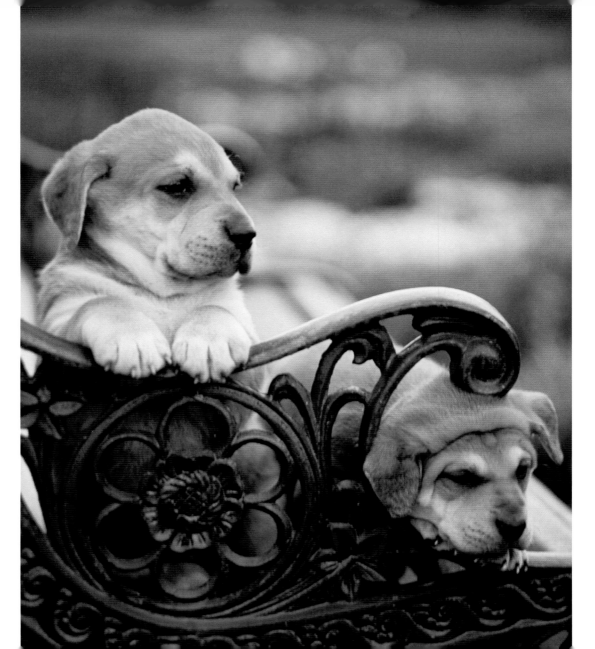

sometimes
a pair.

Maybe 3...

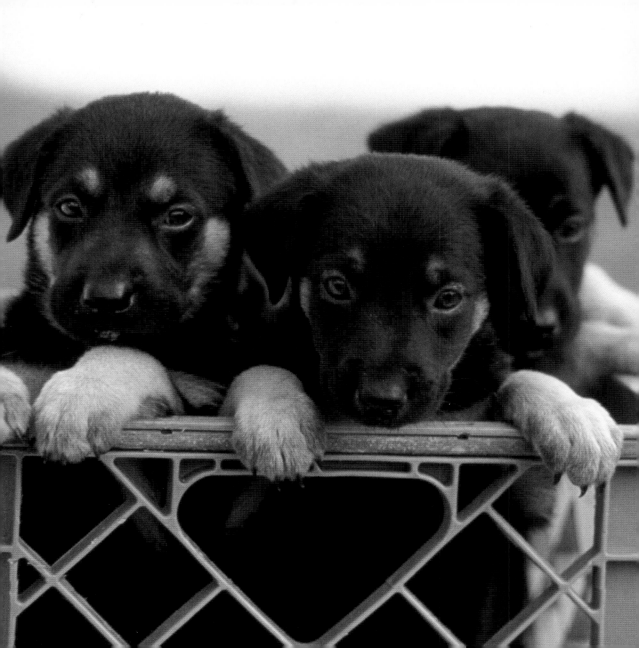

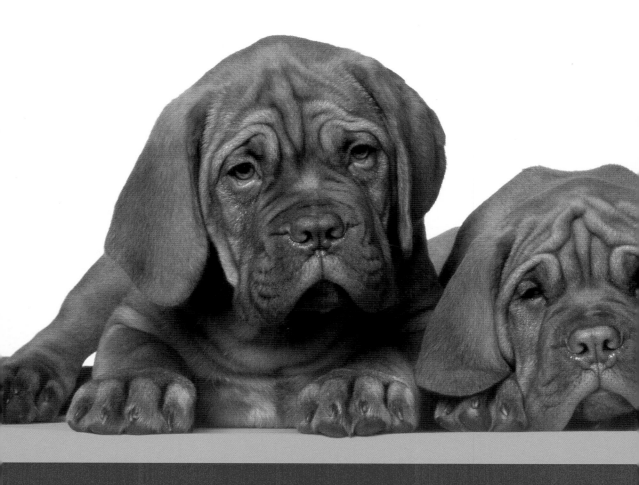

could   there

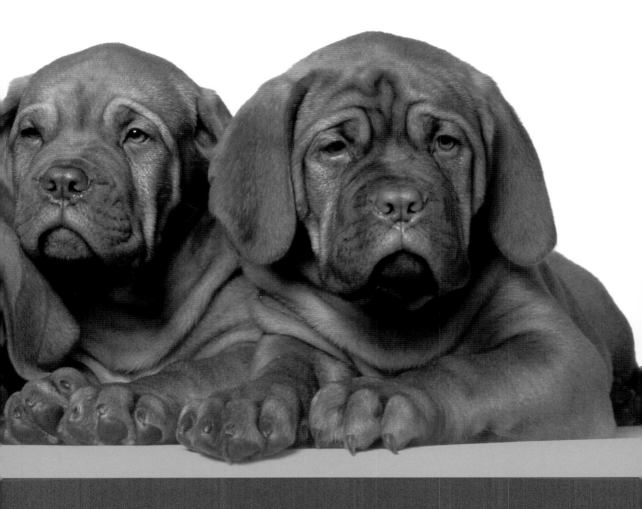

be   four?

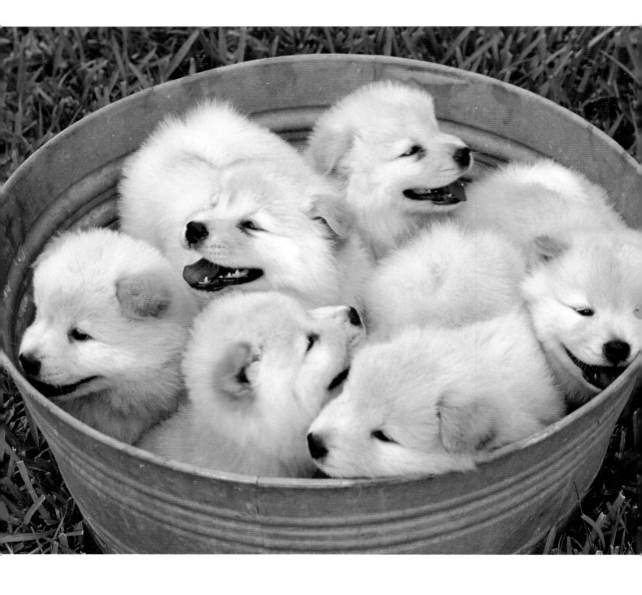

Sometimes many, many more!

BLACK

pup,

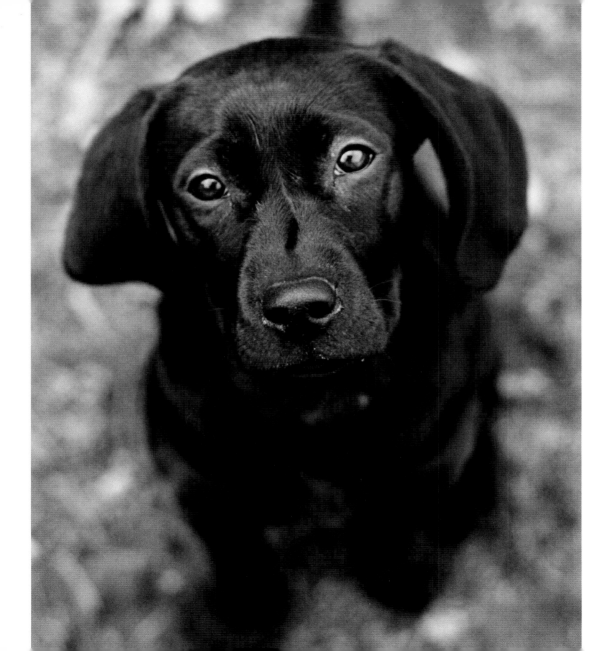

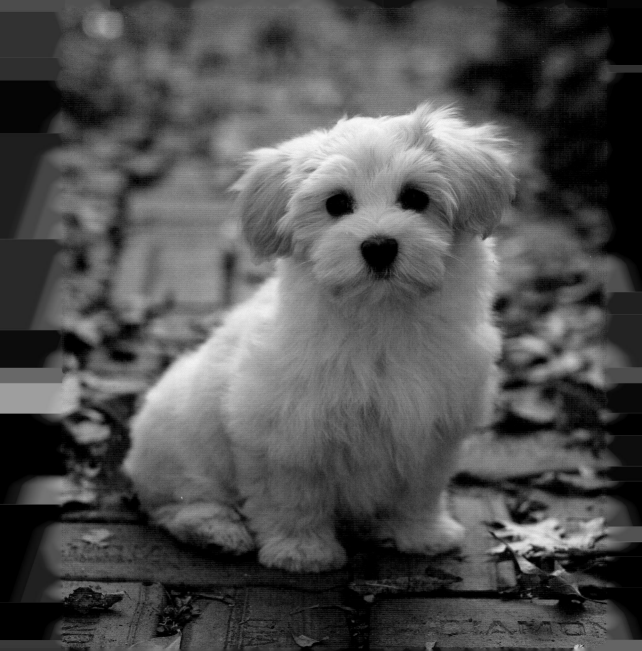

WHITE

pup,

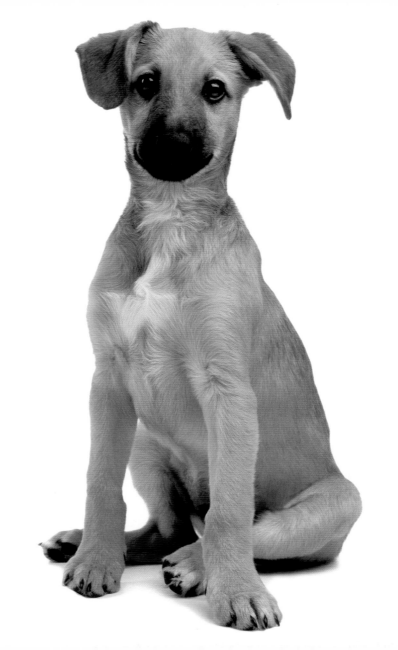

big
pup.

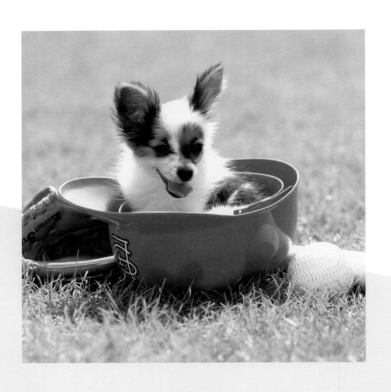

small.

Labrador retriever

Chow   Greyhound   Poodle

Dachshund Great Dane
                                    Boxer
Collie   Weimaraner

Bassett hound

Cocker spaniel   Golden retriever

                                              Pug
Basenji

We don't care—
we like them all.

German shepherd   Siberian husky

Yorkshire terrier

Border collie   Alaskan malamute

                                    Lhasa apso
Newfoundland

Shetland sheepdog
                    Great Pyrenees

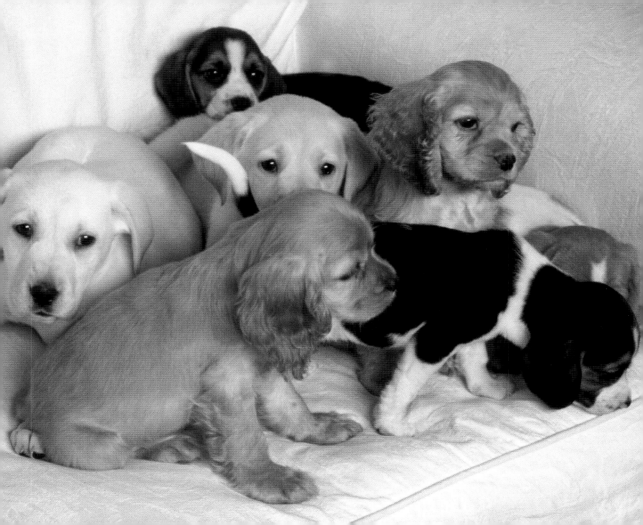

PUREBRED,

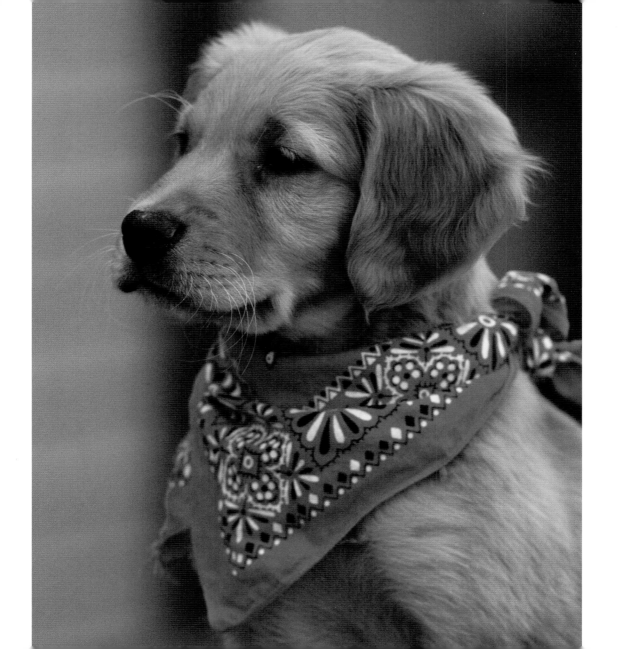

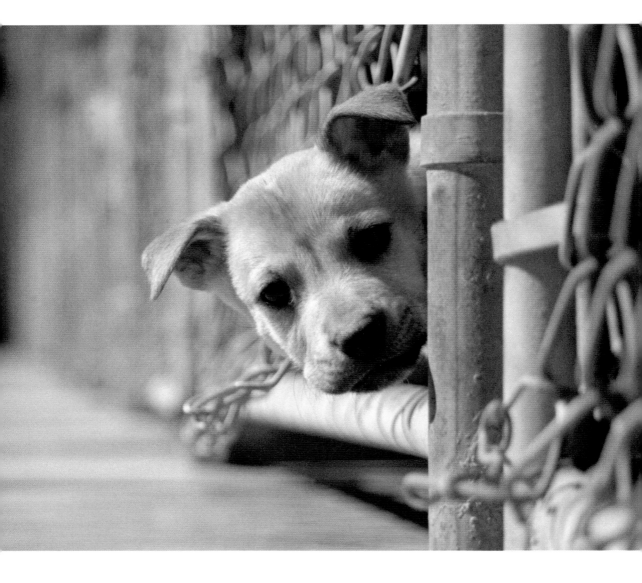

POUND PUP,

doesn't matter—

little
puppies
like to
splatter.

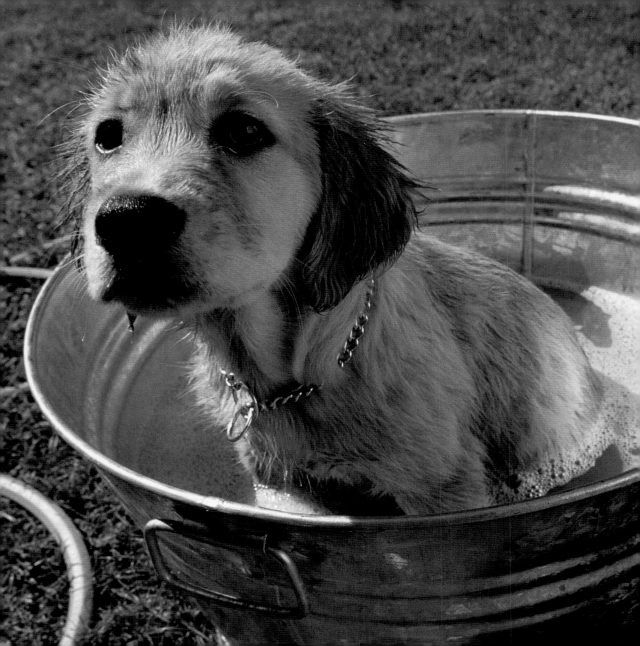

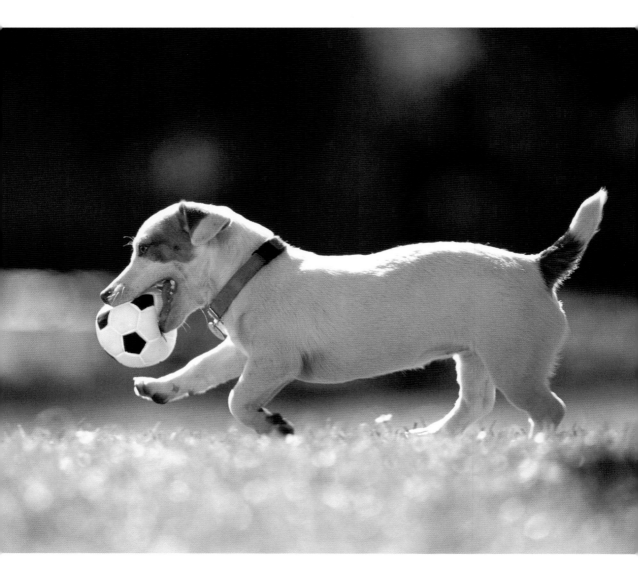

Jingling
trot
across the lawn—

naptime now, after a yawn.

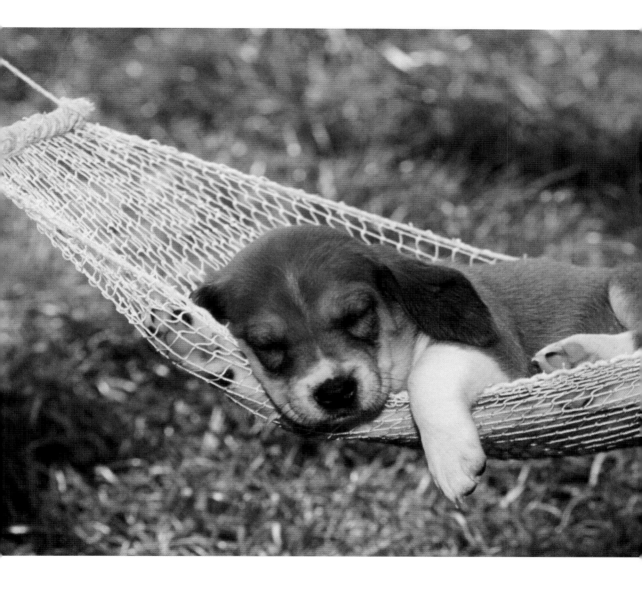

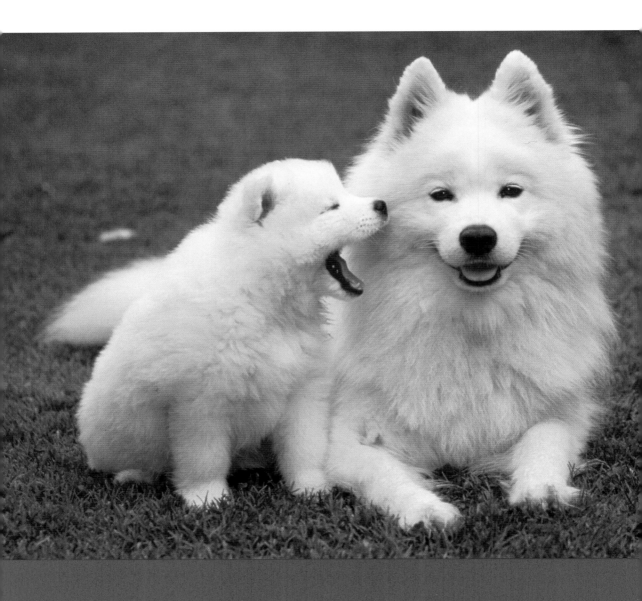

Yipping,

yapping,

sometimes SNAPPING,

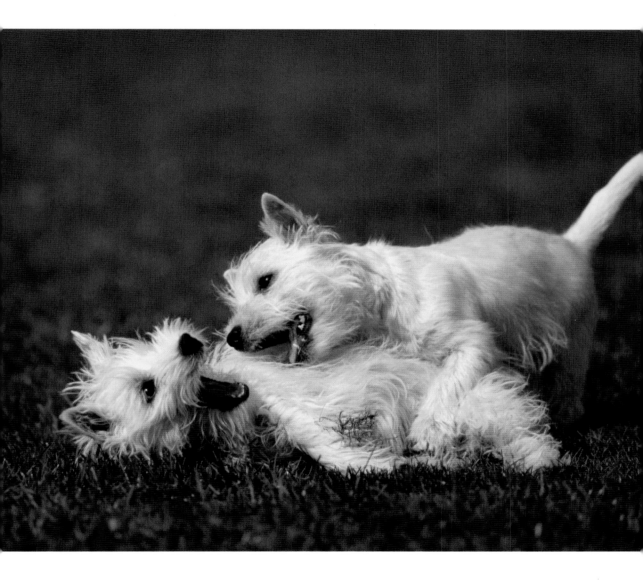

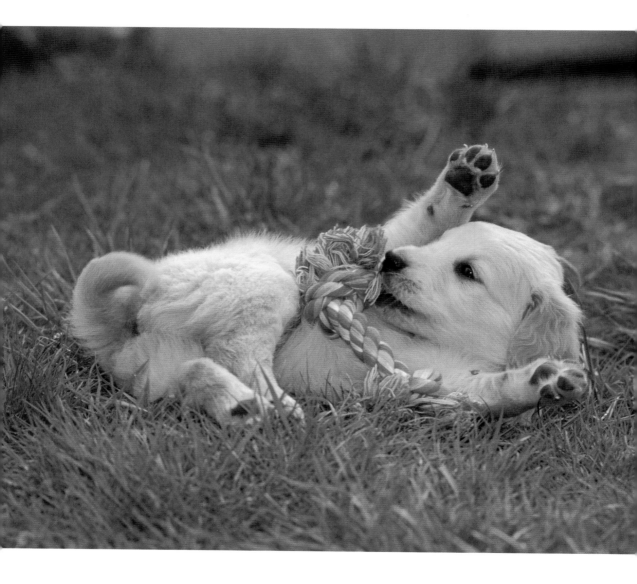

little puppies

having fun.

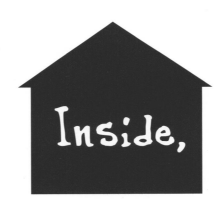

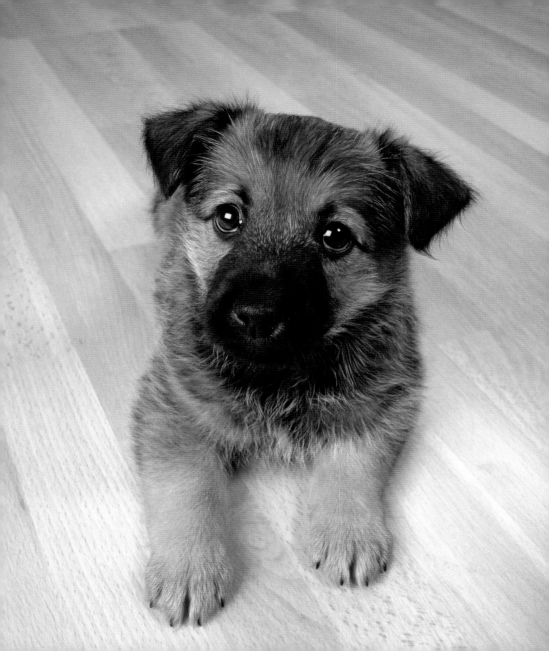

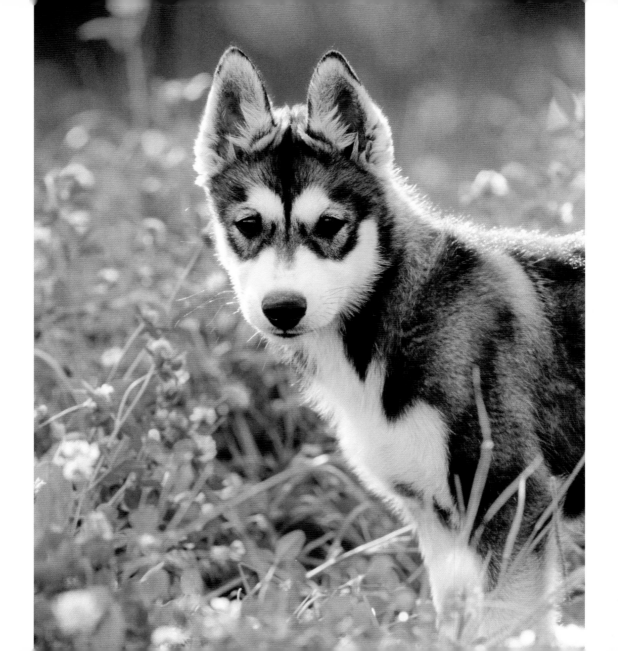

outside,

all around,

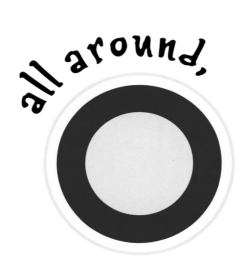

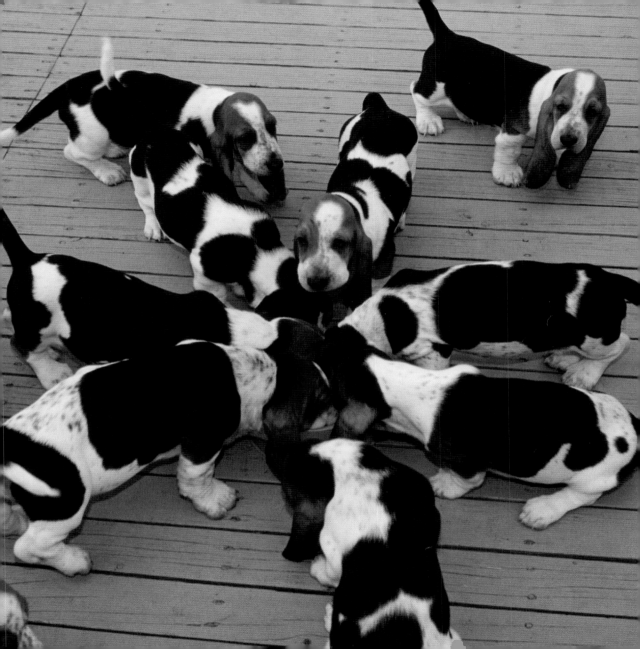

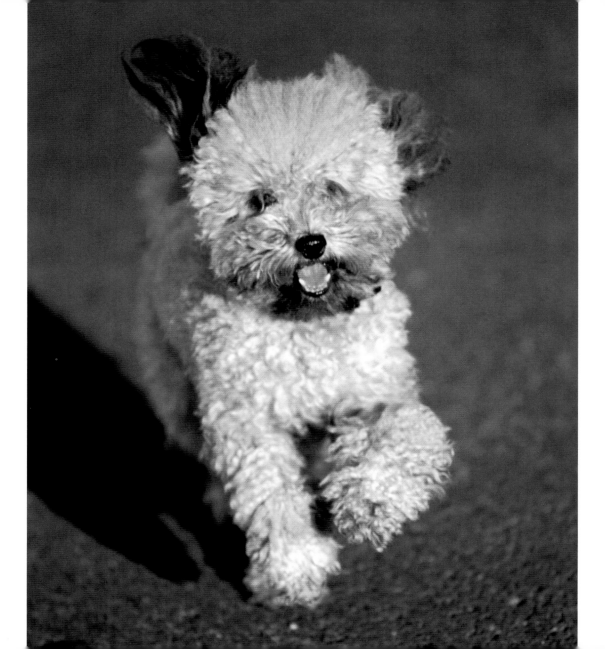

puppies
cover lots
of ground.

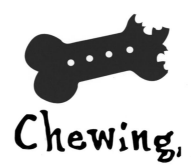

Chewing,

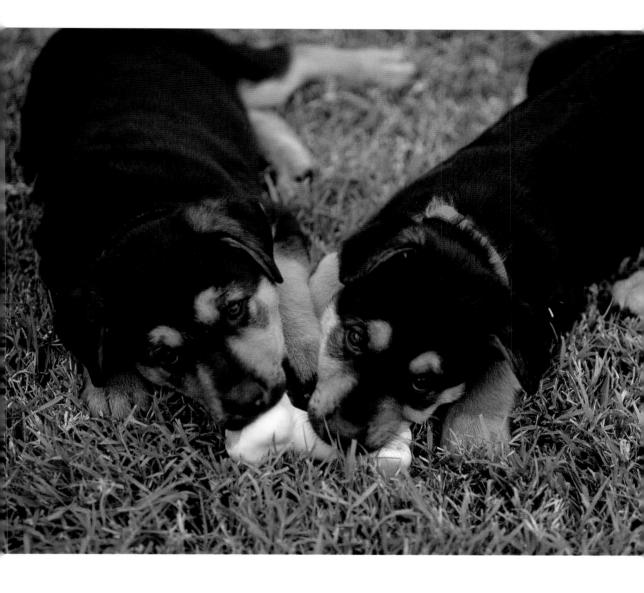

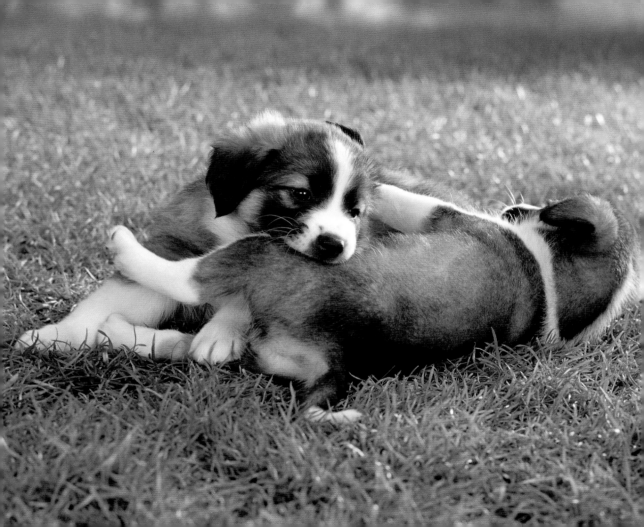

wrestling,

digging holes,

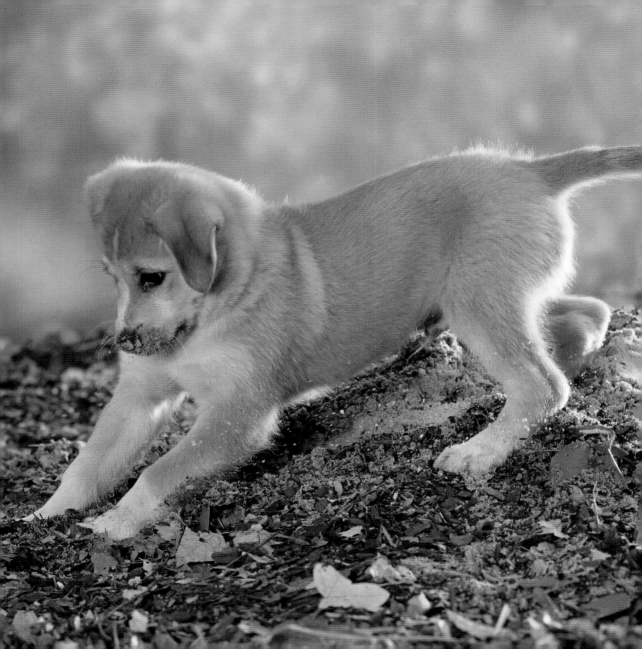

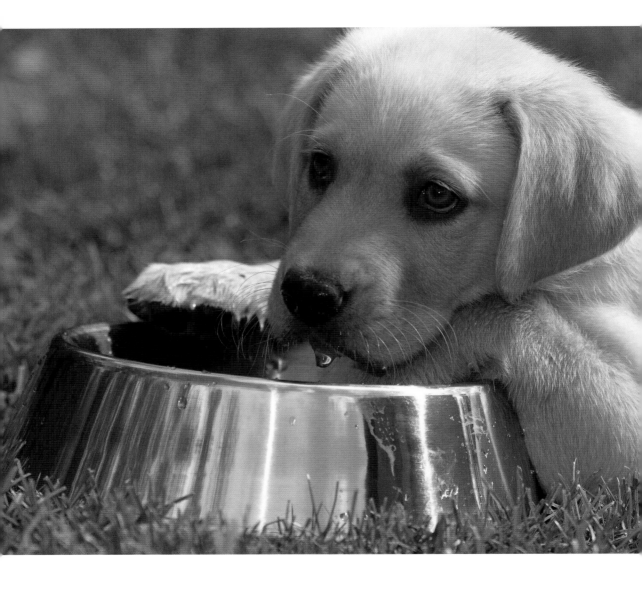

playing
in their water bowls.

Start to leave and they will POUT

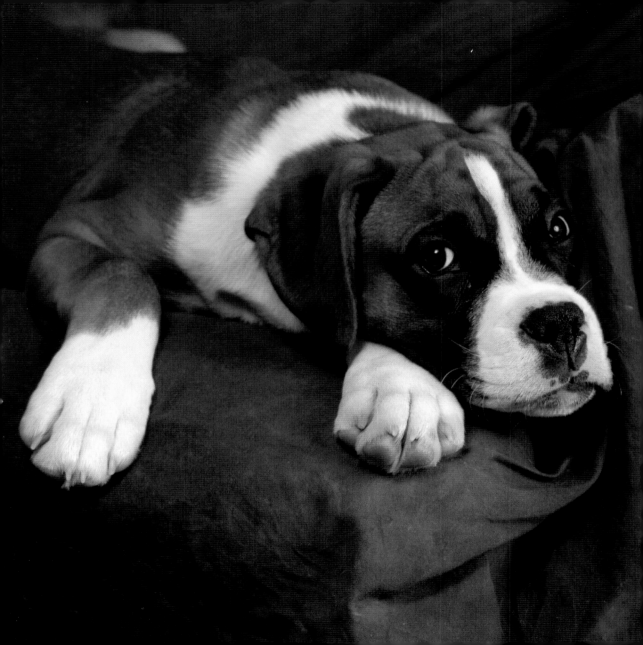

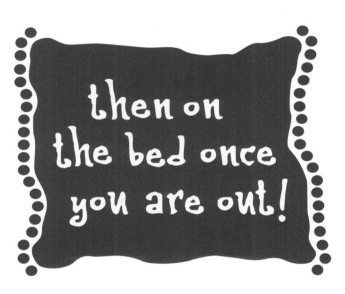
then on
the bed once
you are out!

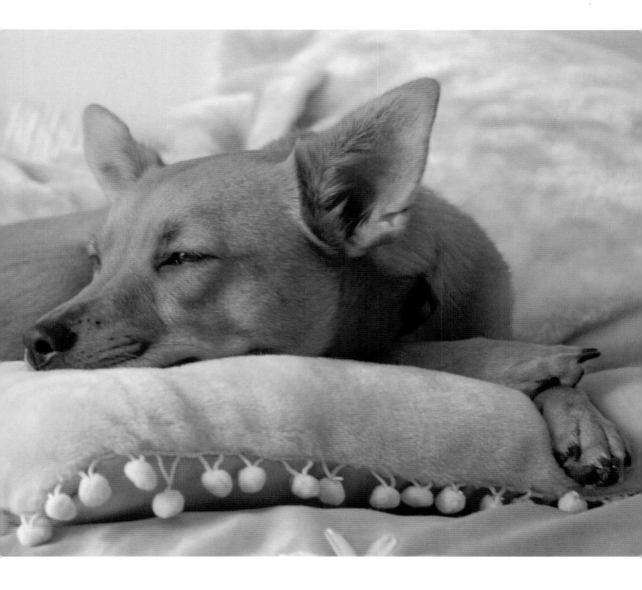

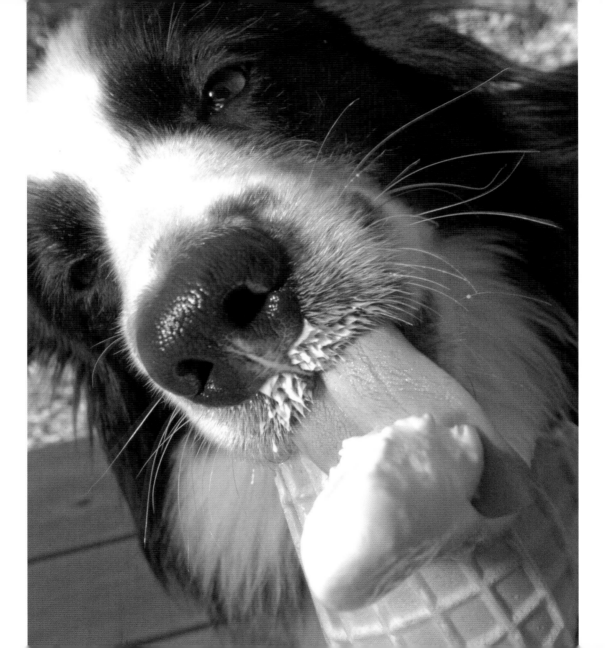

Some pups lick.

some

pups

BARK,

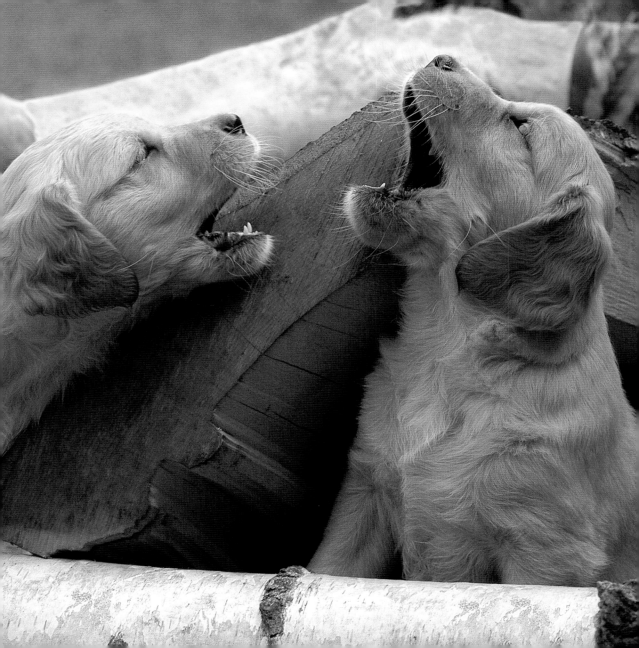

some

tear

everything

apart.

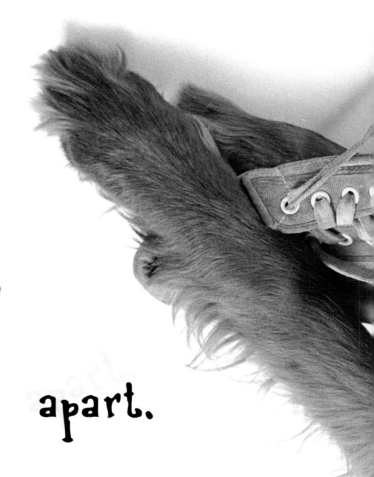

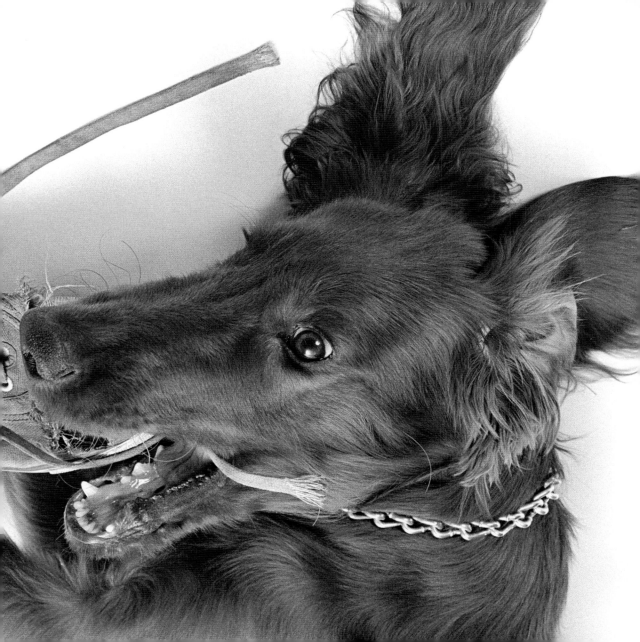

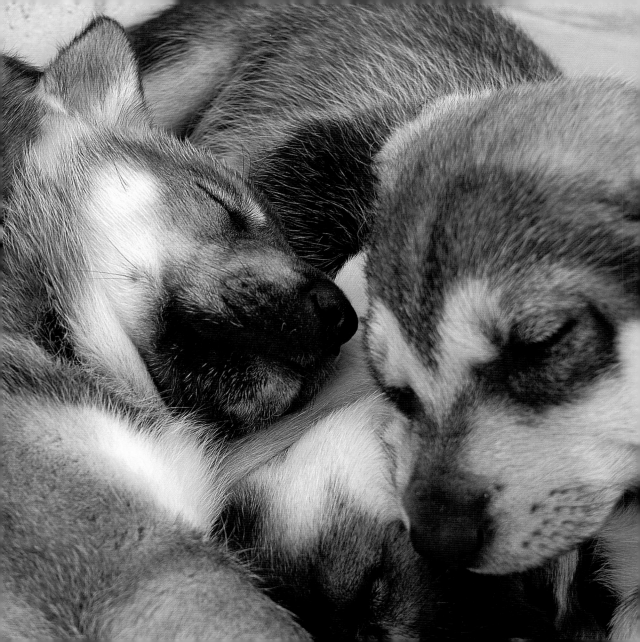

Puppies,
puppies
everywhere—

some of
every kind.

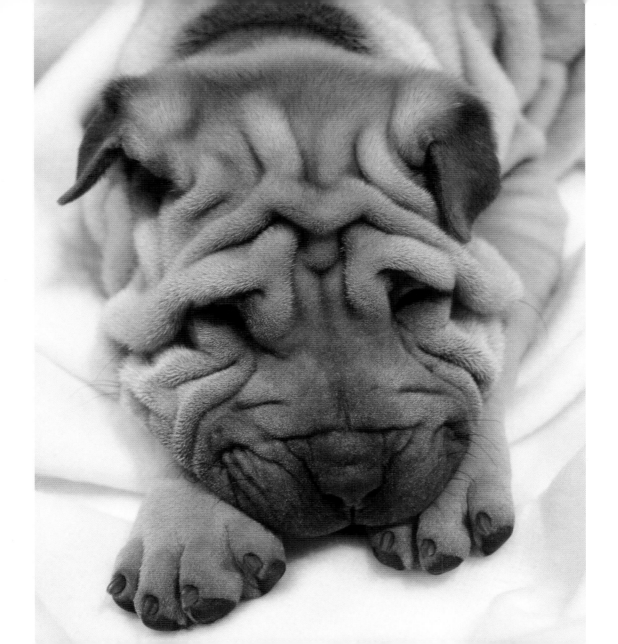

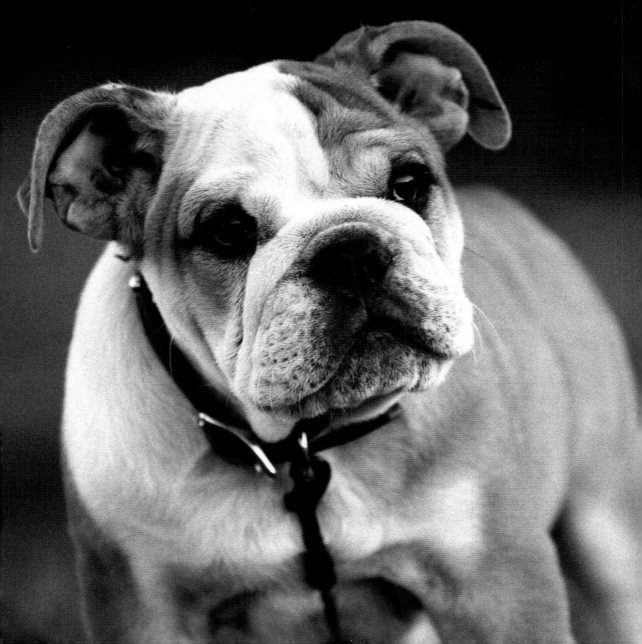

BIG

AND
TOUGH,

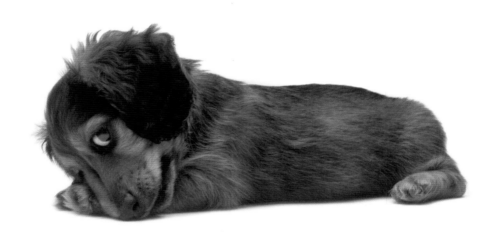

small and shy—

we
like
our
pups
just
fine.

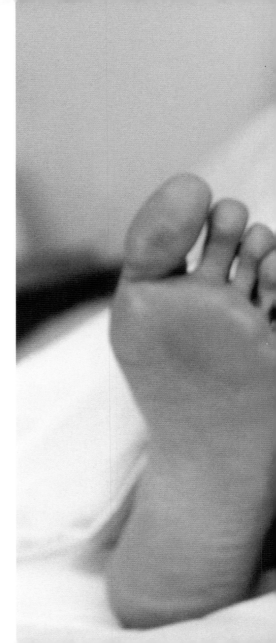

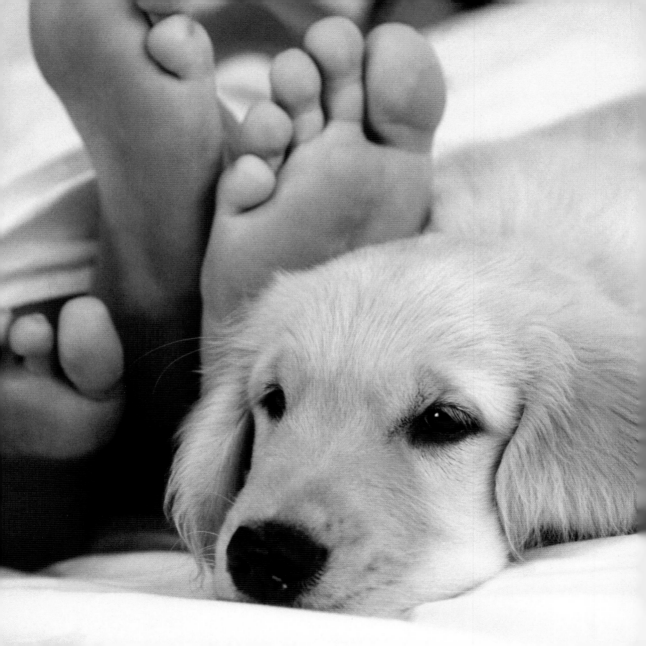

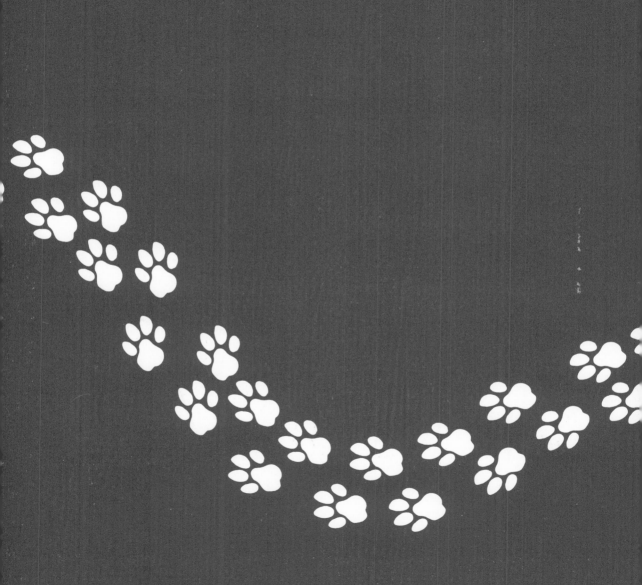

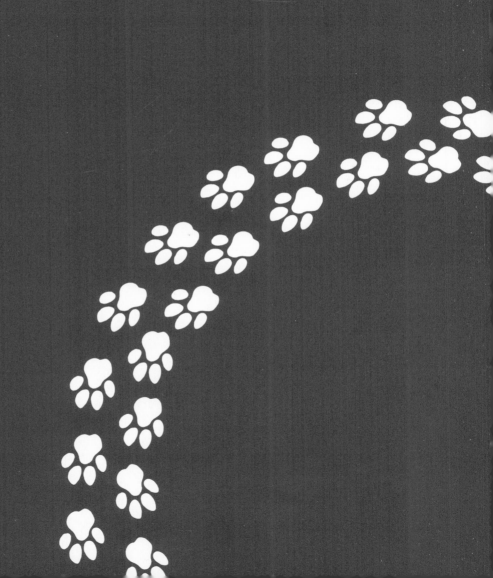